Vancouver Island Birds

by mike yip

volume I

Canadian Cataloguing in Publication Data

Yip, Mike 1943 -
Vancouver Island Birds: a photgraphic
introduction to birds of Vancouver Island
- 1st edition

Includes bibliographic references and index
ISBN 0-9738161-0-4

Mike Yip Publishing
1884 Stewart Road
Nanoose Bay, B.C.
V9P 9E7

http://vancouverislandbirds.com

Printed in Canada

contents

Harlequin Ducks at Qualicum Beach

Prologue

Most people have no idea how many bird species have been observed on Vancouver Island. Although there are no official records, the number is probably over 400. In 2004, an informal tally by the Vancouver Island Yahoo eGroup compiled 312 species for the year. Even in the dead of winter, there are many birds present. On Dec. 18/04, the Victoria Christmas Bird Count established a new Canadian record with 154 species. In any given year, an avid birder should be able to list at least 250 species while diligent recreational birders should get close to 200.

Two years ago my only interest in birds was to prevent the pesky robins from devouring my raspberry crop, and my occasional interest in photography had disap-

Yellow-rumped Warbler at Morningstar

peared when my children abandoned the nest for university. That all changed in February, 2003.

I was enjoying the crisp, sunny morning air as I was driving home to Nanoose from Parksville when a sudden impulse caused me to detour to Wall Beach to watch the sea lions. On the way I was distracted by some ducks grovelling in a secluded marsh. I stopped for a better view through the tangle of willows and reeds. They were about the size and shape of Mallards, but the colour was a little different and they had large, flat spoonbills. I was fascinated and before I realized it, an hour had passed. I couldn't wait to get home to try to identify my discovery. It didn't take long on the internet to find out that they were Northern Shoveler Ducks. I returned the next day with my old

35 mm camera and 85-205 mm zoom lens. The lighting and view was poor, but I shot a roll anyways and headed for Walmart 1-hour photo. I was delighted to have a record of my sighting, but the quality of the photos left much to be desired. For the next 2 weeks I experimented with my old 500 mm barrel lens then a borrowed 400 mm lens with a 2x extender. I crawled along the beach at Nanoose Flats for the Black Oystercatchers. I slithered through the grass in the Nanoose Estuary for Savannah Sparrows, and waited patiently for the Harlequin Ducks at Beachcomber Park. I was amazed at the new birds I found just in my neighbourhood, but I was frustrated at the hundreds of poor photos. I knew I had to get some better equipment. I had to. The discovery of new birds was intoxicating, and I was obsessed with captur-

Ruby-crowned Kinglet at Dolphin Lake

ing their images on film. A week later I went down to London Drugs and spent my daughter's university tuition on a new Nikon F-80 and Sigma 50 - 500 mm lens. For the rest of the year I was like kid with a new toy. I expanded my range south to places like Buttertubs Marsh in Nanaimo, and north to the Englishman Estuary, French Creek, Columbia Beach (Admiral's Lagoon) , and Deep Bay. I hiked Mt. Washington for the American 3-toed Woodpecker, I boated Bamfield for the Tufted Puffin and Red-necked Phalarope, and scoured Clover Point (Victoria) for the Rock Sandpiper and Surfbird. I had a wonderful year exploring the Island and discovering over a 100 wonderful new birds, but I was totally disappointed with the quality of my photos. I had taken over 2000 photos and most of them weren't

worth keeping. I knew I had to go digital. After a few weeks of research and soul-searching, I made my decision. In Feb. 2004, I raided my retirement savings and headed back to London Drugs for a Nikon D-100 digital SLR that would work with my Sigma lens.

Freed from the "negative" economics of film, I went crazy. In the first 2 weeks I took over 2000 pictures. My percentage of quality photos increased dramatically. After about 10,000 pictures in 5 months, there was one last step. Getting close enough to the birds was still a challenge. I knew the pros all used 500 or 600 mm prime lenses with extenders. A little internet research introduced me to the Sigma 300-800 mm lens. I had always liked the flexibility of a zoom lens, and it was considerably cheaper than a prime lens.

Long-tailed Duck at Deep Bay

Rationalizing that "you only live once" and "next year might be too late," I made one last trip to London Drugs and maxed out my credit card. The new lens was monstrous. It weighed 13.5 pounds and was 25 inches long. It was heavy and awkward, but I soon developed a few new muscles, and before long I was back in action. For short hikes, I had no problem carrying the camera and lens on a shoulder strap, but for longer treks, I improvised with an old golf bag and a golf cart. The new lens was amazing, and the quality of my images improved accordingly.

I consider it a privilege and gift to be able to observe, enjoy, and photograph birds, and it has been a pleasure sharing them with bird lovers around the world on my website, http://vancouverislandbirds.com. It is with

the same spirit of sharing that I am producing this book. I know there are many who are unable to enjoy the birds and nature because of work, illness, or other commitments. There is no substitute for the real thing, but a picture can sometimes tell a story, provide the joy of discovery, or even bring a smile to a face.

Unfortunately, bird populations all around the world are endangered by human activity. The situation is no different on Vancouver Island. Species like the Lewis's Woodpecker and Western Bluebird have long been extirpated from the Island, and the Island population of Vesper Sparrows is down to a few breeding pairs. There is little doubt that human activity is directly or indirectly related to the decline of most species. Although it is too late for some birds,

Cedar Waxwing at Buttertubs Marsh

it is critical that we learn from our mistakes and avoid making the same mistakes again. Everything in nature is inter-related and fundamental to basic necessities such as the air we breathe and the water we drink. The extinction of a species is symptomatic of the degradation of our environment. It is not too late to recognize our mistakes and rectify some of the damage we have done. It is a myth that we must continue to destroy our environment in the name of economic development. Nature is a renewable resource that can be managed for the benefit of all. Like the song says, we can "pave paradise and put up a parking lot," or we can enshrine nature, and have people pay us to come and enjoy it.

Please enjoy my photos and love the birds,
Mike
(June, 2005)

shorebirds

Western Sandpipers at Columbia Beach

◎ PEEPS are small sandpipers belonging to the "Calidris" family. They are similar in size and behavior. Locally, they are represented by the Western, Least, and Semipalmated species. Peeps breed in the Arctic and winter in southern states and further south. They are seen on Vancouver Island during migration stop-overs.

Semipalmated Sandpiper at Qualicum Beach

▲ The Semipalmated Sandpiper is the least abundant of the peeps seen on the Island. It generally associates with the other peeps on mudflats or beaches where they forage for food during their spring and fall migration stopovers.

14

Least Sandpiper at Columbia Beach

◄The Least Sandpiper is aptly named as it is the smallest of the three peeps (6.0"). It is also the easiest to identify being the only one with yellow legs. The others are usually black, gray, or dark olive. Another feature is the thin down-curved bill. The Least prefers to forage on grassy or muddy areas and not in the water like other peeps.

Western Sandpiper at French Creek

◄The Western Sandpiper at about 6.5" long, is the largest and most abundant of the three peeps. It usually stands out because of the rufous color on its back and head. In general, it also has the longest and broadest decurved bill. The San Malo Mud Flats and Columbia Beach are two popular feeding areas for the peeps in the Parksville area.

Baird's Sandpiper at Columbia Beach

▲ *Small numbers of Baird's Sandpipers usually visit Vancouver Island during the spring and fall migrations. However, 2004 was unusual as large numbers were seen at places like Holden Creek (Nanaimo) and Tofino. Most of the Baird's migrate through the central flyway of the continent to and from their Arctic breeding grounds.*

▶ *Black Turnstones are common Island residents from August to April. They can usually be found along the rocky coastlines turning over stones and other debris in search of food. In breeding season they head for the northern coast of Alaska and return in late July. The less common Ruddy Turnstone is normally seen only on migration stop-overs.*

Black Turnstone at Columbia Beach

Long-billed Dowitchers at Holden Creek (Nanaimo)

◉ *Long-billed and Short-billed Dowitchers are medium-sized shorebirds with long bills. Their spring and fall migration stop-over schedules are similar to the peeps. They are often found with the peeps on mudflats and shallow ponds. Bill length is not a good identifying feature as there is an overlap in bill sizes.*

◄ *(previous page) Adult Long-billed Dowitchers usually have an entirely rufous belly while the juveniles have gray breasts and plain gray tertials with rusty edges as in the photo to the right and below.*

Long-billed Dowitcher at Holden Creek.

Long-billed Dowitchers at Holden Creek (Nanaimo)

Short-billed Dowitcher at Holden Creek

◄ *The juvenile Short-billed Dowitchers feature dark tertials (long wing feathers) marked by rufous bars as in the photo to the left. (The Short-billed "Dowi" is in the foreground in front of two Longbilled Dowis.) Adult Short-billed Dowitchers usually have orange chests and white bellies. They are also slightly smaller (11") than the Long-billed Dowis (11.5").*

◻ Yellowlegs are also medium-sized shorebirds that stop-over on Vancouver Island during the spring and fall migrations. As the name suggests, the Greater and Lesser Yellowlegs are distinguished by their yellow legs. When seen alone, sometimes they are difficult to identify. However, when seen together, the differences are obvious. The Greater Yellowlegs is the larger bird with an upcurved bill that is longer than its head. In comparison, the Lesser yellowlegs is a smaller bird, and its fairly straight bill is about the same length as its head. The long skinny legs of both species are ideally suited for wading in the shallow waters of tidal pools or ponds where they forage for small fish, tadpoles, insects, other aquatic invertebrates.

Greater Yellowlegs at Viaduct Flats (Victoria)

◄ *The Lesser Yellowlegs averages about 10.5" in length, has a wingspan of about 24," and weighs about 2.8 oz. The Greater Yellowlegs is about 14" long, has a wingspan of 28" and weighs about 6 oz.*
▼   *Lesser Yellowlegs at Holden Creek (Nanaimo).*

Lesser Yellowlegs at Holden Creek

Semipalmated Plover at Columbia Beach

▲ *The Semipalmated Plover looks like a stubby, stunted Killdeer, but unlike the year-round Killdeer, the "Semiplover" is only seen on Vancouver Island during the spring and fall migration stop-overs. The Semiplover is usually found on beaches where it forages for worms and crustaceans after the tide goes out.*

The term "semipalmated" describes the partially webbed feet of the Plover and the similarly named sandpiper. The spring stop-over is usually in April and May while the fall stop-over is in July and August. The Semipalmated Plover has a length of 7.25", wingspan of 19", and weight of 1.6 oz.

Black-bellied Plover
at Oyster Bay

▲ The Black-bellied Plover is a medium-sized shorebird about 11.5' long, with a wingspan of 29", and weight of 8 oz. It nests in the Arctic but winters from Vancouver Island south to Chile. It is commonly found along shorelines, mudflats, and wet fields where it forages for food. The photo above shows the winter plumage which is very plain and dull compared to the distinctive black chest and face of the breeding plumage. While the Black-bellied Plovers are common on Vancouver Island, the Pacific and American Golden-Plovers are quite scarce and only a few are ususally seen on migration stop-overs.

25

Black Oystercatchers & Black Turnstones at Qualicum

◎ *Black Oystercatcher - A fat crow with a carrot bill? You're not dreaming. It's a Black Oystercatcher, a shorebird unique to the west coast of North America. It is a year-round Island resident that hangs out around rocky shorelines. The little ones are Black Turnstones.*

▼ *Spotties - The Spotted Sandpiper or "Spottie" can often be identified by its bobbing action as it sits at the edges of ponds. Although it is sometimes found along the coastal shoreline, it is more frequently seen at freshwater ponds. A few do winter on Vancouver Island, but the majority prefer the warm sun of the southern states and Mexico. The female Spottie is notorious for its infidelity as it is known to mate with several different males. The fathers are left the task of raising the young while the mother is having another affair.*

Spotted Sandpiper at Craig Bay

The Solitary Sandpiper is a medium-sized sandpiper just smaller than a Lesser Yellowlegs. As its name suggests it is generally seen alone or in pairs as it makes its migration stopover on Vancouver Island. It is usually seen on small freshwater-ponds where it feeds on small aquatic invertebrates. Surprisingly, Solitary Sandpipers nest in trees east of the Coast Mountain ranges where they search for abandoned robins, waxwings, or blackbirds' nests. In late summer they head south to the southern states or further to central South America.

Solitary Sandpiper at Craig Bay

▼ *Dunlin are medium-sized sandpipers and the most abundant wintering shorebird on Vancouver Island. Large flocks are frequently seen along the shorelines, beaches, and mudflats where they feed on crustaceans. They are impressive in flight as they soar, dive, and bank synchronously like an aerial ballet. The photo below (taken in Dec.) shows their winter plumage, while the photo on the bottom of the next page (Apr.) shows their breeding plumage.*

Dunlin at San Pareil

Pectoral Sandpiper at Holden Creek

◀ The Pectoral Sandpiper is another medium-sized migratory shorebird seen on its spring and fall stopovers. It generally feeds in wet fields and mudflats where it forages for invertebrates and plant matter. It is known for its unique expanding throat sack that expands and contracts to make a strange mating call.

▼ Dunlin in breeding plumage .

Dunlin at French Creek

▼ *Academy Award Winner - Killdeer are year-round residents famous for their "broken-wing" decoy act to distract danger from their nest and fledglings. They are also very adaptable as they survive* *quite well in habitats from coastal shores to inland farm lands, golf courses, and open fields. Part of their success is due to their protective colouration which blends in very well to their surroundings.*

Killdeer at Columbia Beach

▶ *Invisible Eggs - Killdeer make no effort to conceal their eggs, relying instead one their color and pattern to make them look like rocks and part of the natural environment.*

▲ *Parent Protection - Killdeer parents are always near their fledglings. If the decoy doesn't work, they just hide the babies under them.*

◄ *Walking Cottonballs - Baby Killdeer are amazing as they scoot around like long-legged cottonballs. They have to be fast to survive, but they also are smart enough hide or to stay near their parents.*

Great Blue Heron at Miracle Beach

◄ *Patience Rewarded - The Great Blue Heron stalks its prey by doing nothing. It simply stands motionless, imitating a small tree, waiting for some unsuspecting fish or amphibian to venture within striking distance. The Heron's strike is quick and precise, and the prey becomes the meal.*

Great Blue Heron at Brickyard Bay

◄ *An Appetizer - The prey is juggled around until it is in the right position to be swallowed head-first. Besides fish, the Heron also eats amphibians, snakes, mice, insects, and small birds.*

Great Blue Herons are loners except when they nest together in rookeries. Surprisingly, the largest rookery on Vancouver Island is in Beacon Hill Park in Victoria.

Water Birds

Greater Scaup, Surf Scoters, & Bonaparte Gulls at Qualicum Beach

▼ *Winter Favorites - The artistically coloured ♂ (male) Harlequin Ducks are one of the most admired winter ducks. They are often seen perched on rocks close to the water's edge at low tide. Clover Point in Victoria and Qualicum Beach are popular viewing spots for these attractive ducks.*

In spring the Harlequins head inland to nest at the edges of fast flowing streams. However, once the female starts to incubate the eggs, the males take off, not the least bit ashamed of shirking their paternal duties. The single ♀ (female) parent is left to raise the family on her own.

♀ & ♂ Harlequin Ducks at Qualicum Beach

♂ *Bufflehead Duck at Deep Bay*

♀ *(female) Bufflehead at Deep Bay*

◄▲ The Littlest Duck Buffleheads are the smallest ducks in North America. They are equally adaptable to fresh and salt water where they feed on insects, crustaceans, aquatic invertebrates, and plants. The name Bufflehead is related to its oversized "buffalo" head. Buffleheads are fairly widespread in North America, and nest in trees mainly in central and northern Canada and Alaska.

Class Clowns - The jovial-looking ♂ Surf Scoters are the most numerous of the three Scoter species that frequent the coastal waters. Large flocks of Scoters and other ducks congregate in the Qualicum region to take advantage of the annual mid-island herring spawn. Shortly after, the Scoters depart for their inland breeding grounds in northern Canada and Alaska.

♂ Surf Scoters at Qualicum Beach

Shellfish Lovers - Like all Scoters, the ♀ White-winged Scoter thrives on shellfish. High tide at Qualicum Beach during the winter is a great time to watch them diving for mussels and other shellfish which they swallow - shell and all.

♀ White-winged Scoter at Qualicum

♂ White-winged Scoter at Qualicum

◀ *Punctuation Bird - The ♂ White-winged Scoters are mostly black except for the white comma below the eye , orange and white bill, and white wing patches. The White-winged Scoter is the largest of the three scoters with a length of 21", wingspan of 34", and weight of 3.7 lbs.*

♂ Black Scoter at Qualicum

◀ *Golden Knob - The ♂ Black Scoter is the smallest (19") of the scoter ducks, and easily distinguished by the golden knob on the top of its bill. The ♀ Black Scoter is also reasonably easy to distinguish from the other female scoters as it is the lightest coloured with pale, whitish cheeks, and a smallish, thin bill. Black Scoters are the least patriotic of the scoters as most of them retreat to Alaska for their breeding season.*

Common Merganser family at Englishman River

▲ *Merganser Daycare - The ♀ Common Merganser looks like she's running a daycare on the Englishman River, but the ducklings could be all hers as clutch sizes vary from 1 - 17. It is surprising that such a large bird is a cavity nester.*

▼ *River Runners - Common Mergansers are common on fresh and salt water. They are excellent swimmers and their powerful serrated bills are ideal for snatching fish or even a crayfish from the Little Qualicum River.*

♀ Common Mergansers at Little Qualicum River

▲ *Country Club Birds - A pair of ♂ Common Mergansers were checking out the menu at Fairwinds Golf Club. They weren't impressed with the daily special of "Titlist Pro-V1's".*

▼ *Gourmet Special - The ♂ Red-breasted Merganser found the menu much to his liking at the Brickyard Bay Café. Green eel sushi was the chef's special for the day.*

♂ *Red-breasted Merganser at Brickyard Bay*

▼ *Dolphin Lake Diva - The juvenile Hooded Merganser relaxes with her Yoga stretches in the tranquil confines of Dolphin Lake. Dolphin Lake was the nesting spot for a family of Hooded Mergansers and a family of Wood Ducks in 2004. As cavity nesters, the "Hoodies" may have utilized one of the nest boxes installed by the Nanoose Naturalist Club.*

Juvenile Hooded Merganser at Dolphin Lake

▼ "Hoodies"-Hooded Mergansers are very attractive ducks with the female displaying the latest "Marge Simpson" hairdo and the male sporting the "golf ball" look. Like the other Mergansers, the Hoodies have long , thin serrated bills ideal for grasping their slippery prey. Hoodies are mainly fresh water ducks and quite common on Vancouver Island.

Mr. & Mrs. Hooded Merganser at French Creek

► *Puddle Duck - Mallards are the most common and well-known of the west coast puddle ducks. They are year-round residents and can survive on salt water or even the smallest fresh water pond or puddle. Like most ducks, it is the female that has the chore of raising the family. It is no easy chore as the hyperactive ducklings love to take off and explore on their own.*

♀ *Mallard at Morningstar*

► *Bad Dad - While mother is tending to the family, papa Mallard is apt to be out sewing his wild oats. And, he isn't fussy as he has been known to force his will against ducks of other species. The results, of course, are some interesting hybrids. Despite his unsavory reputation, the attractive male is often the postcard duck for literature and advertising.*

♂ *Mallard at Admiral's Lagoon*

♂ *American Wigeon at Fairwinds*

♂ *Eurasian Wigeon at Fairwinds*

◄▲ *Wigeon Salad - The American Wigeon (above) and the Eurasian Wigeon (left) are vegetarians. The photos show them enjoying aquatic plants at Fairwinds, but they are normally found grazing on the fairways or grassy areas of estuaries. The America Wigeon is one of the most abundant North American Ducks. The Eurasian fugitive from Asia is uncommon but numbers seem to be increasing.*

Long-tailed Duck at Deep Bay

◀ Deep Bay Special - The spit at Deep Bay is an excellent location for winter birding, and its main attraction is the sublime Long-tailed Duck. "Longtails" can usually be seen diving and feeding on mussels just off the spit from November to March. In March, they join the huge flocks of scoters, scaups, and goldeneyes to dine on the protein-rich herring roe from the mid-island herring spawn.

▼ The male has the long tail and pink bill.

Northen Pintails and Green-winged Teal at Holden Creek

▲ "Greyhound of Ducks" - The elegant, slender, long-necked Northern Pintails are a common sight on the Island's estuaries and wetlands from late summer to early spring. They are generally one of the first ducks to leave in the spring and one of the first to return in late summer. Their breeding grounds are extensive, covering north-central U.S., most of Canada, and Alaska.

dant ducks in North America, but drough and loss of habitat has seriously affected their numbers. Northern Pintails average about 21" in length and are just smaller than the Mallard.

Northern Pintails feed mainly on seeds of aquatic plants and small aquatic animals. Like the male Longtail Duck, it is only the male Pintail that sports the long, thir

Northern Shovelers at Holden Creek

▲ *Flat Bills -* *Have you ever seen a Mallard with a stretched and flattened out bill? If you have then you've seen a Northern Shoveler. The oversized bill is designed to act as a scoop and sieve to strain out food (seeds, insects, mollusks, and crustaceans) from the water of shallow marshes and ponds. The Shovelers either feed on floating plants and insects or cause a turbulence with their feet to stir* up food from the bottom of the ponds. *They can also plow through the mud a the bottom of shallow marshes and ponds Some Shovelers do nest on the Island and are present the year-round, but the ma jority tend to head inland and north a far as Alaska. In the winter, the most o Shovelers head for the southern states and Mexico, but a few prefer the friendly con fines of Vancouver Island.*

Goldeneyes are medium-sized ducks that nest in inland tree cavities but spend their winters on coastal, bays, lakes, and rivers. The Common Goldeneye is slightly longer than the Barrow's at 18.5" versus 18" but only weighs 1.9 lb. to the Barrow's 2.1 lb. The two species generally go their separate ways except during the herring spawn when they join the large, mixed flocks of ducks off Qualicum Beach. The Common Goldeneye is widespread across North America while the Barrow's is mainly a West Coast bird with small scattered populations around North America. The male of both species is easily distinguishable by the circular white cheek patch on the Common and the crescent patch on the Barrow's.

Common Goldeneye at Schooner Cove

◀ Mating Games - Two male Common Goldeneye compete for the wing of a female.

▼ Juvenile Barrow's Goldeneye at Schooner Cove.

Common Goldeneyes at Denman Island

Adult ♂ Barrow's at Wall Beach

Juvenile ♂ Barrow's at Schooner Cove

...are the three main items on the dietary list for the Brant that stop-over in the Parksville region on their way north to their Arctic coast breeding grounds in Canada, Alaska, and Russia. Typically, the Brant arrive from late Feb. to early April and are the guests of honor at the Parksville - Qualicum Annual Brant Wildlife Festival. Rathtrevor Beach and Parksville Bay are two excellent venues for viewing the migrating birds.

The Little Sea Goose - Brant are small geese that winter primarily in Mexico and breed in the Canadian and Russian Arctic. On their way north, they stop at strategic locations along the Pacific coast to fuel up on eelgrass and other nutrients such as herring roe in the Parksville - Qualicum region. However, on their way south, they completely bypass the coast and fly directly over the ocean to their wintering grounds in Baja California and Mexico. There are three separate populations of Brant: the western breeding Pacific or Black Brant as described above; the Melville Island breeding Intermediate which winter in Puget Sound, and eastern breeding Pale-bellied that winter on the Atlantic coast.

Brant at Parksville Beach

The Greater White-fronted Goose is an occasional visitor to the Island as it migrates to Alaska and the Arctic coast in the spring and on its return in the fall to the western states and Mexico. It has the most extensive breeding range of any goose as it nests from Russia and all across Alaska and Canada to Greenland. The Greater-white-fronted is a medium-size goose (28") just larger than a Brant. feeds on seeds, grasses, sedges, grain and berries. Like many geese, the Greater white-fronted mates for life, and family units usually migrate together. Its winter habitat is agricultural lands, wetland marshes, and fields.

Greater White-fronted Goose at Fairwinds

Snow Goose at Parksville Park

◄ *The Snow Goose is uncommon on Vancouver Island even though there is a large wintering population on the Fraser River Delta in Ladner. However, the occasional vagrant does drop in to sample Vancouver Island's famous hospitality. Snow Geese nest in the high Arctic where they have endangered themselves by overgrazing their own habitat.*

Cackling Goose at Parksville Park

◄ *A New Species - In 2004 the small Canada Goose came of age and was granted its own status as a separate species from the larger Canada Goose. Several of the small subspecies have been lumped together and are now called Cackling Geese. These include the hutchinsii, asiatica, leucopareia, taverneri, and minima subspecies.*

Tundra & Trumpeter Swans at Somenoes Marsh

Trumpeter Swan on the right was stranded all alone in Somenoes Marsh all winter until a Tundra Swan came to keep it company. Tundra Swans are the smaller species and distinguished by yellow markings on its bill.

▼ Trumpeter Tea Party - The Trumpeters at Mcnabb's farm loved getting together to gossip and socialize at their afternoon tea parties.

Trumpeter Swans at McNabb's Farm

Elegant but Controversial – Mute Swans are not native to North America. They were brought over from Europe as pets or farm birds and then escaped or were released. In 1962, five released birds in Maryland multiplied to over 4,000 and are now seriously affecting the ecosystem by depleting submerged aquatic vegetation and trampling the nesting sites of endangered birds. As the flocks grow on the Island, potential problems can be anticipated.

Mute Swan at Fairwinds

Wilderness Symbol – The haunting wail of the Common Loon is synonymous with the unspoiled northern wilderness. Common Loons are abundant in the secluded offshore waters of the Island from late summer until the spring migration inland and north. Nests are built on quiet shorelines. Some build on floating beds of reeds while others prefer shallow onshore nests close to the water's edge. Two eggs are usually laid and one or two chicks are hatched. It is a classic picture to see a little chick riding on its parents back. By late summer the young are ready to fly and the fall migration to the coast is on.

The Common Loon is a heavy bird requiring a long run to take off but once it is airborne, it is a powerful flyer. Because of its weight, landing is not a graceful event. It is closer to a crash. Despite its lethargic and ponderous looks, the loon is a powerful swimmer.

Common Loon at French Creek

◄ *Sole Food - With a healthy diet of fish and seafood, the Common Loon has no problems with cholesterol. It usually swallows its prey while underwater except for larger items. Larger prey must be killed first, then oriented to be swallowed head-first. Sharing is not part of the loon's vocabulary. If another loon comes close, the one with the food will take evasive action and dive and swim as far and fast as it can to keep the prey for itself. The Common Loon is a powerful swimmer. It folds its wings tightly against its body and propels itself with its large feet. The feet are also essential to help the loon get airborne as it requires a long run before it can fly. However, they are not that useful for walking as they are positioned too far back, and the bird is front heavy. Except when it has an onshore nest close to water, the Common Loon prefers to stay in the water.*

Common Loon at Schooner Cove

▼ ▶ The Red-necked Grebe is a common winter resident of the Island's sheltered offshore waters where it feeds on fish and marine invertebrates. For most of the winter it is a dull muted gray and brown, but as breeding season approaches, it changes its attire into bright spring colours with an attractive rufous neck. Its breeding range is inland from central Canada north into Alaska.

Red-necked Grebe at Deep Bay

Pigeon Guillemot at Deep Bay

▲ The Pigeon Guillemot is a year-round Island bird that is mostly white in the winter and mostly black in the summer. It has distinctive red feet that betrays its identity regardless of plumage.

Pacific Loon at Deep Bay

◄ The Pacific Loon is wary of humans and prefers to stay in flocks with its own kind. In breeding season the lustrous grey head, vertical white neck sripes, and an iridescent purplish neck patch is extremely attractive. In winter, it all disappears to a dull, dark brown and white.

▶ The Pied-billed Grebe is a small diving bird generally found in fresh water ponds, marshes, and lakes. Despite its war-like call, it is a very shy bird that sinks underwater whenever strangers or danger lurks. It is also a very good swimmer, but unlike the webbed feet of ducks, it has lobed toes like a coot. It is a year-round bird on the Island.

▶ The Pied-billed Grebe lays 3 - 10 eggs on a floating platform of grass. Incubation takes just over 3 weeks. The babies are very active and precocious. They are capable of leaving the nest right after hatching and enjoy riding on their parents' backs when danger is near. They have voracious appetites and keep the parents busy feeding them fish, leeches, crayfish, insects and basically anything that they can catch.

Pied-billed Grebe at Buttertubs Marsh

64

Horned Grebe at Brickyard
Bay in breeding plumage

Horned Grebe at Deep Bay

▲ The Horned Grebe is fairly abundant during the winter in the sheltered bays and quiet waters of the Island. Unfortunately, for most of the winter it is in its plain, dull gray and white plumage. It is only near breeding season that it's showtime, and it molts into its spectacular breeding plumage just before it disappears to inland lakes and ponds in central and northern Canada and Alaska. Like the Pied-billed, it builds its nest on floating vegetation and lays 3 - 8 eggs. The chicks are active as soon as they hatch and can swim and dive. However, they remain dependent on their parents for food. Horned Grebes normally eat aquatic insects, fish, crustaceans, and small aquatic animals. A strange habit of the Horned Grebe is plucking and eating its own feathers. One theory is that the feathers function as a plug or filter to aid digestion.

▼ Cormorant Cousins - Cormorants don't seem to mind sharing the same rock as was the case at Chrome Island near Deep Bay. Three Brandt's Cormorants are shown tolerating the presence of the smaller Pelagic Cormorant. The Pelagic is the smallest of the 3 Island species at 28". The Brandt's at 34" is just larger than the Double-crested at 33". The Brandt's is distinguished by a small patch of tan feathers just under the chin, and it also has the shortest tail of the 3 species.

Brandt's & Pelagic Cormorants at Chrome Island

The Double-crested Cormorant has a yellow chin, flies with a kink in its neck, and can be found in salt or fresh water. It is common on the Island and is often seen on pilings or rocks, drying its wings. It is the most abundant cormorant in North America and breeds extensively on both coasts as well as the Great Lakes and the heart of Canada and the U.S. It is an excellent swimmer and primarily a fish eater, but it will also take amphibians, insects, and aquatic animals.

Double-crested Cormorant at French Creek

▼ The Surfbird is common along the Pacific coast from Alaska to Chile during the winter. It is usually seen in flocks, often with Black Turnstones, and the occasional Rock Sandpiper. They all glean invertebrates off the rocks in the intertidal zone and are often referred to as "rock-pipers."

▶ The Common Murre is abundant off the west coast of Vancouver Island where it feeds on fish, squid, and invertebrates. It is a widespread species both in the Pacific and Atlantic. Populations are stable, but vulnerable to oil spills as demonstrated in the early 80's when an oil spill extirpated the species off central California.

rfbirds at Schooner Cove

Common Murre at Bamfield

The Greater Scaup is common on the Island especially during the herring spawn off Qualicum. Flocks of 1000's gather with goldeneye and scoters in an amazing congregation to feast on the bounty of herring roe. Greater Scaup are easily confused with Lesser Scaup, but when the light is right, the male Greater has a greenish sheen while the Lesser has a purplish sheen. The Greater Scaup also has a shorter forehead and a flatter and wider head.

♀ Greater Scaup at Craig Bay

♂ Greater Scaup at Qualicum

American Black Duck at the Crow & Gate

Canvasback at the Crow & Gate

▲ Crow & Gate Duck - The American Black Duck is uncommon on the Island and west coast, but there are often a few in the duck pond at the Crow & Gate pub in Cedar. Its normal range is eastern Canada and U.S.

◄ A surprise visitor this year ('05) at the Crow & Gate has been the ♀ Canvasback. South Vancouver Island is at the northern tip of the Canvasback's winter range. Sightings in the mid-Island are quite uncommon.

The Western Gull is a regular feature on the Island but not in large numbers. With its dark back, white head, heavy bill, and black wingtips, the adult stands out from the flock. But with frequent hybridization and intermediate stages of development, positive identification is never guaranteed. They are more common in Washington and points south.

The Bonaparte Gull is another bird that arrives with the herring spawn at the mid island in early March. It is a small gull with a mostly white head when it arrives but by late April, it is transformed into a Halloween-looking black-headed gull. The Bonaparte breeds inland and after a fall stopover, it moves down the coast for the winter.

Western Gull at Qualicum

Bonaparte Gull at French Creek

Mew Gull at Columbia Beach

◄ The Mew Gull is a common winter resident of the Island. It is considerably smaller (length 16") than the regular Island gulls, and behaves more like a shore bird as it walks around the shallow waters probing for fish, insects, seeds, and invertebrates with it plain thin, yellow bill.

▶ *Bombs Away - The Glaucous-winged Gull opens shells by dropping them on rocks or pavement. It is the most common Island gull and features matching colours on its back and wing-tips.*

▼ *California Dreaming - The California Gull arrives on the mid-Island in large flocks coinciding with the herring spawn. After bulking up with herring roe, it heads for the prairies to breed.*

Glaucous-winged Gull at Columbia Beach

California Gull at Parksville Beach

Heermann's Gull at Clover Point

Ring-billed Gull at Admiral's Lagoon

▲ *California Visitor - The exotic-looking Heermann's Gull winters in California but can be seen in Victoria and the west coast of the Island during the summer.*

◄ *A Ringer - The uncommon Ring-billed Gull is a fairly small gull with a distinctive ringed-bill, yellow eyes, and yellow legs.*

Orange-crowned Warbler at Rathtrevor Park

forest & field birds

■ *Early Birds - Rufous Hummingbirds are among the first summer migrants to arrive on the Island from their winter vacations in Mexico. Males generally arrive by the third week in March and the females follow a few days later. The female builds the nest and raises the babies. The male is only involved with the fun stuff..*

Rufous Hummingbird in Nanoose

▲ ► *In the mid and south Island, the Rufous mate by early April and after 2 weeks of incubation and 3 weeks of daycare, newly fledged youngsters begin to appear by mid-May. They are a joy to watch at backyard feeders.*

◄ The female Rufous has a green back and a small gorget (throat feathers).

▼ The male Rufous has an orange back and a full glistening gorget which serves both as a warning and attraction sign.

▲ Long Distant Champ - Ounce for ounce, the Rufous Hummingbird holds the record for the greatest migration distance travelled per ounce of bird. The Arctic Tern may travel a greater distance but not in terms of miles per ounce. Some Rufous migrate from Mexico to Alaska or about 3,600 miles. But at a weight of of 0.12 oz, that translates to 30,000 miles per oz.

The Arctic Tern travels about 12,500 miles but weighs 3.6 oz. for a miles to weight ratio of about 3,500 miles per oz. It's not even close.

Humans have studied hummingbirds to learn a few things about flight. Perhaps it would be wise to analyze hummingbirds to learn the secrets about their fuel efficiency.

Northern Flicker at Fairwinds

▲ The Northern Flicker is a beautifully marked woodpecker slightly larger than a robin. Although it is often seen on trees, it is more commonly on the ground feeding on ants with its long, sticky tongue. When it is drumming on hollow trees, rooftops, or chimneys, it is actually a female trying to attract a male for a mate. The Flicker above is probably a hybrid as the red malar (moustache) is a trait of the Red-shafted, and the red nape is a trait of the Yellow-shafted population.

Red-breasted Sapsucker at River's Edge

▲ The Red-breasted Sapsucker is a medium-sized woodpecker often mistaken for the eastern Red-headed Woodpecker. However, it is a distinct species and as the name suggests, it specializes in sipping sap from parallel rows of shallow holes it drills in the bark of trees. The Sapsucker returns later to drink the sap and dine on any insects that might have gotten stuck in the sticky substance. Sapsuckers move to coastal areas in the winter but prefer mid-elevations for the summer.

Bald Eagle at Qualicum Beach

Fledgling Bald Eagle at Dolphin Lake

◄ **Monarchs of the Island** - The majestic Bald Eagle is truly the royalty of birds as it surveys its domain from tree-top thrones. Fish is the favorite food for the Bald Eagle, but a stray gosling, a careless gull, a sea lion carcass, dead livestock or small pets will also suffice. It takes four years for young eagles to mature into adults.

▲ **Ready to Rumble** - After 5 weeks in the egg and 10 - 12 weeks in the nest by Dolphin Lake, junior and his sister were ready to take on the world. They had to as their parents had stopped feeding them. The parents tempted them by flying close with food. That would be the reward after the first flight.

▲ *Deep Bay Dinner - A sea lion carcass at Deep Bay (Jan. 2004) provided ample nutrition for the 2nd year Bald Eagle. Adult Bald Eagles continue to feed their young usually up to their first winter. After that the juveniles are on their own. For the first month or two after fledging, the juveniles must practice soaring and finding prey, but they still rely on their parents for food until they develop their hunting skills. If it is a tough winter, many will not survive.*

Merlin at Holden Creek

▲ *Terrors of the Marsh - If you ever see a flock of shorebirds scatter, look for a Merlin, a small (10"), dark falcon. Merlin also pursue small birds like House Finches, and they have a playful side as they play tag with the crows. On a quiet summer day on a marsh, they can often be seen cruising around and snatching dragonflies out of the air. Although the Pacific variety of the Merlin is very dark, winter usually brings in a few of the lighter Taiga and Prairie subspecies.*

▼ The Cowichan Osprey - Ospreys are universal birds, found all over the world. They are amazing fishers. As they spot their prey from high in the air, they hover, then dive feet first, totally submerging from the momentum of the dive. There is a lull as you wonder where it is, then suddenly there is an explosion of spray as the Osprey catapults from the depths with its prey firmly attached to its powerful talons. With the shortage of appropriate nesting trees, Osprey are relying on human assistance as in the case at Cowichan Bay where a nesting platform has been utilized by a pair of Osprey. They will also use hydro poles.

Osprey at Cowichan Bay

▼ *Redtails in the Sunset - As the name suggests, most forms of the adult Red-tailed Hawk have a rufous red tail, and it is the most abundant hawk on the Island. It is found almost everywhere: farmlands, open fields, suburbia, and along the Island Highway. Its most common hunting strategy is to to sit and wait for some small mammal, reptile, or bird to stray into its sight before swooping down for the kill.*

Populations of the Red-tailed Hawk appear to be stable across North America which may suggest that it has benefitted from increased farmland, clear-cutting, and development.

Redtail Hawk at Parksville

Great Horned Owl in Nanoose

▲ *Night Bird - Owls are generally heard and not seen because of their nocturnal preferences. However, juvenile Great Horned Owls like the one above have big appetites and sometimes can't wait till dark. The great Horned Owl will eat practically anything that moves including crows and skunks. Fortunately, there are no skunks on the Island, but there is an abundance of "Sooke" bunnies much to the liking of the Great Horned. Other dietary items include cats, amphibians, rats, nestling Osprey and Falcons, and other owls. The Great Horned Owl in turn is the often harassed by crows that will pester them for hours.*

Cooper's Hawk at Fairwinds

Sharp-shinned Hawk at craig Bay

▲ Despite the distribution maps in certain bird guides, many Cooper's Hawks do winter on the Island, particularly in the Victoria region. The Cooper's often careens recklessly through the bushes after its prey at the risk of injury to itself. Studies have shown a high percentage of birds do suffer fairly serious injuries like broken bones.

▲ The Sharp-shinned Hawk is very similar but slightly smaller than the Cooper's. However, a large "Sharpie" can easily be the size of a small Coopers which confuses the identification picture even more. Sharpies have acquired the reputation as feeder birds, not for the bird seed, but for the birds that feed there.

▼ *Mates for Life - The Common Raven may not be so common these days when broken marriages seem like the norm. Like the Bald Eagle, the Ravens engage in a spectacular aerial courtship of locked claws and tumbling freefall that is breathtaking to witness. Ravens are territorial and year-round residents of the Island. They are often seen by roadsides dining on roadkill.*

Common Ravens at Deep Bay

Turkey Vulture at Nanoose Bay

▲ Thermal Rider - Turkey Vultures are weak flyers and actually rely on thermals to carry them across the straits to and from the Island. Like many Canadian "Snowbirds," Turkey Vultures winter in California and Mexico.

◀ Life's a Beach - The Northwestern Crow is often seen at the beach scavenging for seafood, but it will eat anything including human garbage.

91

▼ Brood Parasitism is the phenomena of one bird laying its eggs in the nests of other birds. The Brown-headed Cowbird is guilty of this behavior with disastrous results for some species. Some species are capable of recognizing the alien egg and removing or destroying it. However, when the egg isn't removed, the result is predictable. The larger Cowbird chick dominates the nest and hogs the food to the detriment of the other species. As illustrated below, the dedicated Yellow-rumped parent is run ragged trying to appease the appetite of its alien foster child.

Brood parasitism at Sproat Lake

Brewer's Blackbird
at Whiffen Spit

◀ *Urbanized Bird - Al-though Brewer's Black-birds can ususally be found on farmlands and marshes, they have adapted well to civilization. They are now common in parking lots like Woodgrove centre in Na-naimo. Their normal food is insects, but like the rest of us, they don't mind a bit of junk food.*

Redwing Blackbird at Dolphin Lake

◀*King of the Bulrushes - Wherever you find bul-rushes, you'll usually find Redwing Blackbirds. The females are brown streaked birds that blend in well with the habitat where they nest, while the male is a handsome black with a flashy red arm patch. The males are polygamus and commandeer their harems in their section of the marsh. Although some Redwings winter on the Island, the majority move south into the states.*

93

Savannah Sparrow at Nanoose Estuary

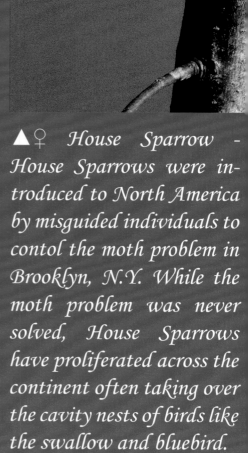

▲ *Savannah Sparrows are summer migrants arriving on the Island in March and April. They are usually found in open fields where they feed on seeds and insects. They are easily distinguishable by the yellow strip above the eye. Although the occasional bird lingers through the winter, most head for the southern states.*

▲♀ *House Sparrow - House Sparrows were introduced to North America by misguided individuals to contol the moth problem in Brooklyn, N.Y. While the moth problem was never solved, House Sparrows have proliferated across the continent often taking over the cavity nests of birds like the swallow and bluebird.*

94

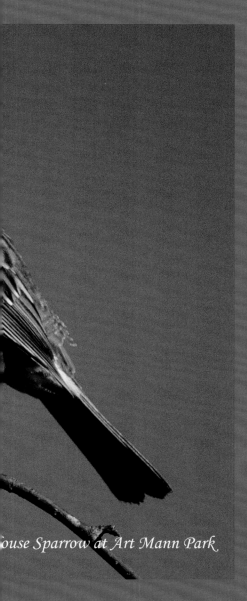

ouse Sparrow at Art Mann Park

White Crowned Sparrow at Springford's Farm

▲ *White-crowned Spar-rows are seen year-round on the Island, but they are migratory. The birds we see during the winter have ac-tually migrated from more northern locations while our summer birds have gone south. Mature birds are easily recognized by their white and black crowns while immature birds have rusty crowns.*

95

▼ *Year-round Songster* - *Like those of us on minimal incomes, the Song Sparrow does not migrate for the winter. We are blessed with their presence all year and there is nothing more pleasing on a cold winter's day than the beautiful notes of the prolific Song Sparrow. It is commonly seen around ponds, hedgerows, thickets, forests, and gardens where it feeds on seeds and insects. "Prolific' also refers to its mating and reproduction as it can raise up to three or four families a year. It has a very efficient arrangement where the male raises the family while the female prepares for the next brood.*

Song Sparrow at French Creek.

▼ The Sewing Machine - Like a well-oiled sewing machine, the gentle trill from the Island forests signals the April return of the Chipping Sparrows from their Mexican vacations. With its rufous crown and and brown back streaks on a light grayish body, the Chipping Sparrow is usually easy to identify.

The Chipping Sparrow builds a flimsy nest in an evergreen tree where the female lays her four eggs. With incubation and fledging completed in less than four weeks, a second brood is usually produced. The main diet of the Chpping Sparrow consists of seeds but it is also supplemented by insects.

Chipping Sparrow at Parksville

► *Sly as a Fox - Fox Sparrows are aptly named after the rufous tones of the eastern cousins, but a case can also be made for the way this year-round bird sneaks out of the underbrush looking for food. Blackberry thickets are favorite hiding spots, but it can be attracted to backyard feeders particularly if snow is covering the ground. A pattern of upside down "v's" on a white chest is a prominent identifying feature.*

Fox Sparrow at Columbia Beach

► *The Lincoln's Sparrow resembles a Song Sparrow with a buffy breast. Although a few winter on the Island, most are seen in April and May and then in September and October on their migration stops. Unlike some species, the Lincoln's has adapted quite well to clear-cut forests and their numbers appear to be on the rise.*

Lincoln's Sparrow at Eaglecrest

House Finch at French Creek

◄ House Finches are year-round residents of the Island. While the females are plain, gray-streaked birds, the males are flashy with their orangey red bibs and foreheads. (Some variants have yellow instead of red.) Apparently females are attracted to the reddest males. House Finches have adapted well to suburbia, and their populations are stable.

Gold-crowned Sparrow at San Pareil

◄ Mr. Big - The Gold-crowned is the largest of the Isalnd sparrows averaging 7.25" in length. (White-crowned and Fox Sparrows are about 7.0".) Gold-crowns are year-round birds, but they move to higher elevations for the breeding season. The gold-crown and bi-coloured bill are unmistakable identifying features. Immature birds without the gold crown can be identified by the bi-coloured bill.

► Like House Finches, Purple Finches are year-round residents of the Island, but they prefer forests, parks, and rural settings to suburbia. The ♂ Purple Finch has deeper and shinier red than the House Finch.

▼ The American Goldfinch is one of the most recognizable birds on the Island. It winters in the southern states but is seen on the Island from spring to late fall. Thistle seeds are one of its favorite foods.

Purple Finch at Nanoose

American Goldfinch at Cottonwood

Yellow-rumped Warbler at Morningstar

▲ The attractive Yellow-rumped war- bler is one of the earliest arriving summer migrants. After wintering in Mexico and Central America, it usually starts return- ing to the Island by early March. It can often be seen hawking insects from trees besides lakes or ponds. There are two sub- species of the Yellow-rumped. The Audubon's has a yellow throat patch and is found mainly in the west. The Myrtle's has a white throat patch (as in the above photo) and is more widespread and more common in the east. Despite being vic- timized by the brood parasitism of the Brown-headed Cowbird, Yellow-rumped populations are not endangered.

▼ Western Tanagers winter in Mexico and Central America but breed in the western states and western Canada as far north as the southern parts of Alaska and the Territories. The male is a spectacular looking bird with a bright red head on a yellow body. Females are attractive in their own right with olive-yellow bodies.

Western Tanagers subsist mainly on insects and fruit. They can be attracted to backyard feeders with fresh and dried fruit. The red pigmentation of the male's head is related the the insects in its diet. The Tanagers usually choose conifers like Douglas firs for their nesting .

Western Tanager at Nile Creek

Yellow Warbler at Buttertubs Marsh

◄ Candy-striper - A brilliant yellow bird with red chest stripes is unmistakeably a ♂ Yellow Warbler. It is fairly widespread across the U.S and Canada and starts showing on the Island in April after a lengthy journey from Central and South America. Its breeding range extends north to the Arctic and Alaska.

Wilson's Warbler at Nile Creek

◄ The Wilson's Warbler is a small, secretive bird, but always a treat to see. At first glance the bright yellow face and chest may seem like a Yellow Warbler but the unique black skull cap is definitive for a Wilson's. The Wilson's is difficult to see as it prefers the cover of dense bushes and vegetation near water.

103

► The Bewick's Wren is a year-round resident on the Island. It is mainly a western and southwestern bird in North America as eastern populations have declined drastically. The Bewick's loves to hide in thick brush and blackberry thickets but also enjoys singing from the tip of a branch or the high part of the thicket.

Bewick's Wren at French Creek

► The Nest-maker - The loud, raspy chatter at any bulrush marsh is a sure sign of the Marsh Wren. However, locating the bird can be a difficult chore. First of all, it usually stays low in the thick bulrushes. Secondly, it is a master ventriloquist and its sound seems to come from several different directions. The male Marsh Wren loves to build nests - perhaps to distract predators or to attract females. The irony is that the female only lays in the nest of her own making.

Marsh Wren at Whiffen Spit

American Pipit at Nile Creek

▲ The American Pipit looks like a sparrow with a thin bill. It is common in coastal areas during the winter but spends the summers at higher elevations where it nests. Its nest consists of a shallow scrape in the ground away from the prevailing winds. The courting behavior of the male is interesting as he sails high into the air them flutters gently back to earth.

After the breeding season, the Pipit returns to the coastal lowlands and fields where it forages for seeds and insects. The word "pipit" is onomatopoetic as it resembles the sound made by the bird. Although some Pipits do overwinter on the Island, most move southward down the coast to the southern states, Mexico, and central America.

Olive-sided Flycatcher at River's Edge

▲ The Olive-sided Flycatcher comes all the way from South America to breed and dine on the Island insects. During the summer it can often be seen perched on the top of tall trees where it flies back and forth collecting insects for its meal. It has benefitted from burned forests, clear-cuts and land clearing providing there are a few snags and trees left. Unfortunately, populations are in serious decline possibly because of disturbances of their wintering grounds.

Willow Flycatcher at Legacy Marsh

◄ The unmistakeable "fitz-bew" emanating from deciduous forests signals the presence of the Willow Flycatcher. Characteristically, it flies out from its perch, catches its prey, and returns to the same perch. The Willow usually arrives to the Island in late April and early May from its winter home in Mexico, Central America, or South America. North Vancouver Island is at the northern tip of its breeding range.

◄ The Hammond Flycatcher is slightly smaller than the Willow and generally prefers conifers where it finds it prey of caterpillars and insects. It has a smaller bill and is more olive coloured than the Willow. Its breeding range extends north into the heart of Alaska, and it winters in Mexico and Central America.

Hammond's Flycatcher at Arrowsmith

▼ *Winter Beauty - The Varied Thrush looks like a robin designed by Picasso with its randomly distributed colourful orange markings. It is a year-round Island resident, but in winter, the population explodes with an influx of northern migrants. Like the Robin, it is a type of thrush. It is a very shy bird that prefers the cover of the forest. However, like an achilles, food will draw it to backyard feeders and gardens especially during harsh conditions like freezing temperatures and deep snow. Its diet consists of fruits, nuts, seeds, and arthropods. In the fall it is often seen with large flocks of Robins descending into arbutus trees to dine on arbutus berries. Its presence in the forest is betrayed by its pleasing single note song followed by a higher or lower pitch. As summer nears, the varied Thrush heads north or up the mountains for their breeding season.*

Varied Thrush at Nanoose Bay

◄ The well-known American Robin needs no introduction.

▼ The Swainson's Thrush is a very secretive summer migrant from central and South America. Its beautiful song is often heard but it is seldom seen during its short summer stay.

Swaison's Thrush at Craig Bay

109

▼ *Woodland Delight - The Ruby-crowned Kinglet is a delightful little bird that never stops moving as it searches for insects in trees or flies out and catches them in the air. It is a year-round bird on the Island but most of the population migrates south down the Pacific coast for the winter. The name, Ruby-crowned is derived from the gorgeous, bright ruby crown sported by the male. The ruby crown is especially visible when the bird is excited and the crown feathers are raised. Females are once again discriminated against and do not have the ruby crown. An amazing fact is that the female lays 5 - 11 eggs and the weight of the eggs can be equal to her own weight. The eggs are incubated for about 12 days and the chicks are fledged in another 12.*

Ruby-crowned Kinglet at Dolphin Lake

Hutton's Vireo at Nile Creek

▲ The Hutton's Vireo is a year-round Island resident that resembles a female ruby-crowned Kinglet. However, the Hutton's is slightly larger (4.5") with a thicker, hooked bill and it is usually not as active. The Hutton's diet consists mainly of insects and spiders, and its preferred habitat is evergreen forests. The male and female Hutton's are similar. They build a cup nest at the horizontal fork near the end of a branch and 4 eggs are laid. The eggs are incubated for 2 weeks and 2 weeks later, the babies are fledged. The Hutton's Vireo is strictly a western bird with a range that extends down the west coast to Central America. Because of the geographic variations in the range, there are about 12 different subspecies.

111

▼ ► *Western Meadowlarks are uncommon year-round birds on the Island, but there is an increase from September to April during the migration periods. They are more commonly found in the Okanagan and east to the southern prairies.*

Western Meadowlark at Nanoose Bay

Bullock's Oriole at Buttertub's Marsh

▲ *Buttertubs' Special* - One of the annual birding treats of Nanaimo is the pair of Bullock's Orioles at Buttertubs Marsh. They are very uncommon summer migrants to the Island with only a few sighted each year. However, they are a spectacular-looking bird and a joy to see when they arrive. They build hanging nests woven from hair, twine, fibers, and grasses. They also build dummy nests to distract predators. Their diet includes caterpillars, fruit, insects, and spiders. The Bullock's normal breeding range is the southern interior of B.C. and south through central and western states. They winter in Mexico and Central America.

▼ *Alcoholics? - Cedar Waxwings are attractive with their smooth yellowish feathers, black mask, red wingtips and yellow tailtips. They eat insects but are also very fond of fruit such as Hawthorne berries and wild crabapples. In fact, the love of fruit is sometimes their downfall as they have been known to expire from alcohol poisoning thanks to fermented fruit. They are fairly widespread across Canada and the U.S. during the summer and some do winter on the Island.*

Cedar Waxwing at Buttertub's Marsh

◄ *Upside Down Bird - The Red-breasted Nuthatch seems to spend most of its time in a downward position as it prefers to go down trees head-first. It is widespread across Canada and a year-round bird on the Island. Its diet consists of spiders, insects, and conifer seeds. It is also fond of sunflower seeds from backyard feeders.*

Red-breasted Nuthatch at Nanoose

◄ *Dark-eyed Juncos are one of the most abundant birds across the country. They are common at backyard feeders and have a preference for white millet. On the Island, the main subspecies is the Oregon which has a black hood and brown back. The photo shows a cross between an Oregon and a Slate-coloured Junco. Most Juncos head to higher elevations for breeding, but a few do breed at lower levels.*

Dark-eyed Junco at Nanoose

♂ Black-headed Grosbeak at Legacy Marsh

▲ ♂ Black-headed Grosbeak - Despite having the flashy good looks of a playboy, the male has been well-domesticated and shares equally the duties of raising the family. Being at the northern tip of the breeding range, Island populations are not widespread or abundant. Male Black-headed Grosbeaks take two years to develop their adult plumage. Yearlings that are close to full development are usually capable of defending their own territory and breeding.

♀ *Black-headed Grosbeak at Legacy Marsh*

▲ ♀ *Black-headed Grosbeak - Apparently, the female Grosbeak loves to sing. In fact, she sings the male's song. Speculation has it that she does it to deceive the male, forcing him to stick around to check out who the competition is.*

Grosbeaks eat insects, seeds, and fruit and can be attracted to backyard feeders. The female lays 2 - 5 eggs and incubation takes about 12 days. It takes another 12 days to fledge. Black-headed Grosbeaks spend their winters in Mexico.

Common Nighthawk at River's Edge

▲ *Not a Hawk - The Common Nighthawk is a member of the nightjar family which are night-flying insect eaters. Nighthawks winter in South America and are widespread across Canada and the U.S. in the summer breeding season, but their populations have decreased drastically in some locations. Their earth tone colours pro-* *vide excellent protective colouration both for when they sleeping during the day on a horizontal branch or a gravel roof, and when they are on the ground for nesting. Nighthawks are known for their amazing power dives and sudden braking which produces a sound like a vibrating rubber band.*

♀ *Purple Martin at Nanoose*

◄ ♀ *Purple Martin - Purple Martins spend their winters in South America. Older Martins start arriving on the Island in early April, and the yearlings follow 4 - 6 weeks later. They are commonly seen at marinas or at the waterfront where nest boxes have been placed.*

♂ *Purple Martin at Nanoose Flats*

◄ ♂ *Purple Martin - Purple Martins are the largest birds of the swallow family. They measure about 8" long compared to the Barn Swallow at 6.75". Most of the other swallows are less than 6" long.*

◉ *Artificial Housing - All of the known Purple Martin on the Island nest in nest boxes provided by humans. Populations in B.C. crashed in the 40's coinciding with increase in Starlings and the decrease in nesting cavities. By the 80's, only a few breeding pairs were left. Apparently, only an aggressive nest box program prevented the extipation of Purple Martins from B.C. Nest boxes have now been installed at many marinas and old foreshore pilings along the east coast of the Island, and the population seems to be increasing steadily. The transition from natural cavities to man-made housing is an example of a "behavior tradition shift."*

▶ *Tee Time? - Black terns are fresh water terns and rare visitors to Vancouver Island. Their normal summer breeding range extends from central B.C. to eastern Canada. Their winter home is the north coast of South America. On Aug. 25/04, a Black Tern appeared on the pond at the 18th fairway of Fairwinds Golf Course and took advantage of Fairwinds' hospitality for seven days.*

rare & uncommon birds

Black Tern at Fairwinds

► *Lark Sparrows are rare on the Island as the northwestern extemity of their breeding range is normally southern Oregon. However, a vagrant visited San Malo Crescent on Nov. 23/04 for about 5 days.*

▼ *Long-billed Curlew nest in central B.C. and are rare on the coast. There were 2 in Tofino from about Aug. 1 - 14/04.*

Lark Sparrow at San Malo Mud Flats

Long-billed Curlew at Tofino

Gret Egret at San Malo Mud Flats

▲ The Great Egret at San Malo mud flats was one of several on the Island in the summer of 2004. Their normal summer range is Oregon and points south and east.

◄ A King Eider Duck was spotted at Fanny Bay in Feb. 2004. It stayed in the area until late April, well after the herring spawn.

King Eider at Fanny Bay

123

► Lapland Longspurs breed on the Arctic tundra and winter in southern Canada and the U.S. Only a few seem to stop on the Island on their southward migration. Photo: Deep Bay, Oct. 20/04

▼ Rock Wren are common in the Interior and points south. In 2003 only one was reported on the Island and that was at French Creek. In 2004 there was one confirmed sighting in Parksville and several in Victoria. Photo: Victoria, Oct. 11/04

Lapland Longspur at Deep Bay

Rock Wren in Victoria

◄ *Grasshopper Sparrows normally breed in the southern Okanagan and south through eastern Washington and Oregon before heading south to the southern states and Mexico. It was a rare find to discover one on Whiffin Spit (Sooke) in the third week of November 2004.*

Grasshopper Sparrow at Whiffin Spit

◄ *The Black-crowned Night-Heron has an extensive range but it normally doesn't include Vancouver Island. The only sighting in 2004 was in mid-August near Ucluelet. Its breeding range extends up through Washington and its winter range is in Mexico to South America.*

Black Crown Night-Heron at Ucluelet

INDEX

Bibliography

Baron, Nancy and Acorn, John. *Birds of Coastal British Columbia and the Pacific Northwest.* Vancouver: Lone Pine Publishing, 1997.

Sibley, David Allen. *National Audubon Society The Sibley Guide to Birds.* New York: Alfred A. Knopf, Inc., 2000

Internet Resources

Cornell Lab of Ornithology. All About Birds ,Online Bird Guide. *http://birds.cornell.edu.* Cornell Lab of Ornithology, 2003

USGS Patuxent Wildlife Research Center. Patuxent Bird identification Infocenter. *http://mbr-pwr.usgs.gov/infocenter/infocenter.html.* USGS, 2000

Dedication

To my wife, Kathleen, who has always tolerated and supported my obsessions including my current passion for birds and photography.

The Last Word

The beauty of producing my own book is that I can do whatever I like, including having the last word.

I wish I had more images to share with you, but my compact flash card is pretty well empty. You now have the best of my first two years of birding and my first year of digital photography. Of course, I will continue to take photos, but finding new birds has become exponentially more difficult. There may be over 400 birds that have been reported in Vancouver Island, but the chances of ever seeing them all is impossible. 300 would be a challenge even for a full-time birder. Photography is another matter. I'm aiming for 200 in 5 years. I have presented 124 birds in this book. If I get 76 more, "Vancouver Island Birds, volume II" just might happen.

In the meantime, I hope I have introduced a few people to a fascinating new world. It is a world that we all share but too often take for granted. It is a world that is integral to the very air we breathe and water we drink, but we often treat it with disdain and recklessness. It is a world that we must learn more about and care more about. Learning about birds is an enjoyable and interesting way of learning about our natural world. Learning about birds will give insights into the functioning of ecosystems and the damage being done to them. It is not too late to learn, and if we each do our share, the birds and nature just might have a chance.

All the best,
Mike

▶ *preview - vol. II*